Let's Visit the Zoo

by
Kate Morgan

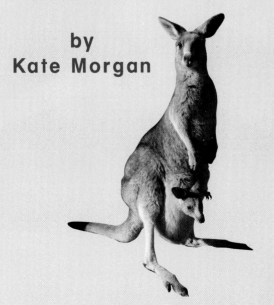

 **Harcourt**

Orlando Boston Dallas Chicago San Diego

Visit *The Learning Site!*

www.harcourtschool.com

Look at the monkeys.
Monkeys have long tails.

Look at the zebras.
Zebras have black and
white stripes.

Look at the elephants.
Elephants have very long
noses.

Look at the polar bears.
Polar bears have white fur.

Look at the giraffes.
Giraffes have very long
necks.

Look at the lions.
Lions have fur around their faces.

Look at the crocodiles.
Crocodiles have lots of
teeth.

Look at the ostriches.
Ostriches have very
skinny legs.

Look at the kangaroos.
Kangaroos have pouches
for their babies.

Look at the camels.
Camels have humps on
their backs.

Look at the leopards.
Leopards have spots on
their fur.